Start Your Wealth Building Now

Revealing Concepts to Investing Made Simple

By Anthony R. Thomas

Legal & Disclaimer

The information contained in this book is not
designed to replace or take the place of any form of
professional advice. The information in this book
has been provided for educational purposes only.

The information contained in this book has been
compiled from sources deemed reliable, and it is
accurate to the best of the Author's knowledge;
however, the Author cannot guarantee its accuracy
and validity and cannot be held liable for any errors
or omissions. Changes are periodically made to this
book. You must get professional medical advice
before using any of the suggested techniques, or
information in this book.

Upon using the information contained in this book,
you agree to hold harmless the Author from and
against any damages, costs, and expenses, including
any legal fees potentially resulting from the
application of any of the information provided by
this guide. This disclaimer applies to any damages
or injury caused by the use and application, whether

directly or indirectly, of any advice or information presented, whether for breach of contract, tort, negligence, personal injury, criminal intent, or under any other cause of action.

You agree to accept all risks of using the information presented inside this book.

Table of Contents

Introduction

When I started my first job, back when I was only 22 years old, a colleague of mine who had been working a few years longer than me asked me if I was investing in my 401K (a retirement savings system in the US). I said, "I am not eligible until I am here for 6 months. "She said, "Good!! Let me tell you what you should do." It was a short conversation in the hall-way and I listened although I am sure I did not fully comprehend. I did sign up for the 401K and started to save and invest based on her recommendations. This was the start of my wealth creation.

I was lucky. I made good friends with people who had some knowledge about how and why to save money and how to invest that money so when I retire it would have grown sufficiently that my family will have enough to live on without having to work. Did I say I was lucky? I look back on some of those "happen-stances" I had when I was younger and the tips I heard, stored back in my brain, and had them retrieved when I needed them or whenever I felt they made sense.

I now realize that it is these basic principles that actually work - 1) you need to save, 2) you need to save as much as you can, 3) you have to buy what

1

you need and try to minimize buying what you want, and 4) you ought to learn how to grow your savings so your money works for you and you do not work for the money. I also made an observation that many people (I guesstimate 80% or more of them) are generally not really that good with money. I attribute it to two simple hypothesis - 1) most people are not that great with or afraid of math (or at least money math) or 2) most people are just afraid to set a budget for themselves. Overcoming these fears and setting a budget is where you need start to be successful in your own personal wealth creation.

The *"Effective Investment Strategies: Your Guide to Income Generation and Wealth Accumulation "* will provide you a better understanding of what lures people to become wealthy and step by step instructions on how you can start building wealth on your own. It includes my personal accounts, clear illustrations on how the strategies can be applied, and examples on how the examples have enriched other people.

Every chapter of the book was organized and worded so it will be understood even by those who have just started with their career, business venture, or whatever form of living you have chosen to take.

There's no point in delaying, the sooner you start getting to know these techniques, the sooner your wealth will begin growing. Start learning how you can make your way to achieving financial success today.

Chapter 1:

Wealth Creation – One of Man's Innate Desires

Let's face it, anything that promises wealth has a powerful way of attracting people's attention. Common marketing lines such as "become a millionaire", "your way to build a fortune", and "live a luxurious life" draw readers into at least making inquiries, if not signing up or purchasing the product, business, or service being promoted.

One may ask then, "Why does wealth and synonymous ideas like glamour, prosperity, abundance, high-end, luxury, & being rich, lure people in so much they desire to achieve it?"

In describing man's conscious and unconscious desires and forces, For Dummies describes the Austrian neurologist and Father of Psychoanalysis, Sigmund Freud, believing that people are mere actors in the drama of their minds and are "pushed by desire and pulled by conscience."

As I researched different materials to find out what really keeps humans to want more money and wealth, I came up with a list of these three main themes: freedom, fame, and power.

4

1.   Freedom

People long for wealth to achieve two kinds of freedom: personal and financial. Greatly influenced by commercialism, the desire comes from the objective of being finally liberated from certain boundaries and limitations of acquiring materials and achieving a certain status in life. Living on a meager budget, people would someday want to achieve any or a combination of the following:

a.   *Personal Freedom*

1.   Experience luxury – People who have limited possessions and life experiences dream of getting the chance to buy the latest gadgets, wear signature and trendy shoes and clothes, eat in expensive and fancy restaurants, go on pleasure trips throughout the world, and know how it feels to live a high-end lifestyle.

2.   Live comfortably - Wealth comes with the ability to own or temporarily stay in spacious and luxurious estates and facilities. Enjoy the first class services and amenities that come with the high-end accommodations. The ability to buy vehicles, expensive furniture, and modern appliances which can do chores or make things with just one click of a button or turn of a switch.

3.   Pursue Dreams – Empowered by substantial resources, the intention of finishing a course, giving financial aid to family members, friends or charitable institutions, provide the best education for children, creating an impressive real estate property portfolio, having all the necessary health, life, and non-life insurances that are available. The basic desire of getting into a more pleasant environment and out of the slums or depressed communities finally becomes a reality.

b.   *Financial Freedom*

1. Choose how you work or if you work - Affluence gives you the choice between working (to accumulate more wealth) or to fully enjoy the fruits of your earlier hard work.

2. Escape from the "paycheck to paycheck " way of living - Since you no longer "have to work", you also no longer have to live within by a salary, make a budget out of what's left from the last paycheck, or wait for the next paycheck to cover unpaid bills.

3. Use debt to make money not to borrow money - As you make financial progress, there is no longer the need for you to acquire debts or apply for loans to pay for items like a car or your own home. In fact, it may now

be you who has the capacity to grant these privileges or borrow money in order to earn money from your existing wealth.

2.   For Fame

With the acquired wealth comes a change in one's status in the society. We have witnessed countless tales of people who rose from "rags to riches" and they have commonly enjoyed the following:

a. Become a public figure – Wealthy people have become individuals who are easily recognized and acknowledged in place, and can use their status to help make a difference in the world.

b. Enjoy people's attention and admiration – By becoming a public figure, the wealthy ones usually find people staring and observing them in great awe. Some of them are invited to give inspirational talks, to do interviews, or even become the subject of their own success story books.

c. Establish a status symbol – The style and brand of shoes, apparel, cars and almost every possession that wealthy people have turn out to be very coveted and become objects of desire. This can be turned into

7

attracting people who want to own a piece of what you are wearing or using to become your own successful brand.

3.   For Power

It has long been known and accepted that whoever holds the money has the power. In an office, for instance, the budget manager has a big say in the company's purchases and projects. The same goes for our society where the wealthy people enjoy clout and influence on certain decisions and actions. Due to their experiences, these wealthy people are also recognized as authorities on subject matters dealing with financial success, wealth accumulation, and property ownership & management.

Everyone will have their own reason for wanting to create wealth for themselves and their families. I believe that if your focus is mostly on #1 Freedom, you are doing it for the right reasons and you will increase your chances for success. #2 Fame and #3 Power usually are an outcome from your desire for financial independence. Another scenario can be that Fame or Power are the motivation driving you to succeed with your financial goals.   My experience has taught me that if you do not let Fame or Power go to your head, you will be very

8

successful. If you do not take heed on managing your desire for Fame or Power you can lose the wealth you worked so hard to create more quickly than you gained it in the first place.

Chapter 2:

People Work Hard yet Most Still Live Paycheck to Paycheck – Why?

Early this year, a major daily newspaper in the United States reported a survey result released by the Sun Trust, with the survey conducted by Harris Poll , revealing that about one third of American households earning between $75,000 to $100,000 annually, live paycheck to paycheck.

You may be confused by such a figure and begin to wonder where could the problem lie, considering that the US is already an economic superpower? What is the percentage of people living in poorer countries? It should be obvious that not only the Americans find themselves in this situation. In fact, most people are now working more than eight hours a day and yet barely breaking even at the end of the month. Expenses are the same or greater than the salary, making many people living at or below the poverty level, has become world-wide malady today.

As I listen to people tell why they suffer this problem, the following are the main factors that prevent them from accumulating wealth.

10

1.   High cost of living

This appears to be the most obvious reason, but I don't think it is the primary cause. Take the case of a middle-income couple with kids and without a house of their own. On top of their expenses for their basic needs, they may have to hire a baby sitter to look after their children while they are at work along with paying for their rent, utilities, auto loan, and health insurance, which makes it difficult for them to make ends meet.

2.   Negative thoughts

a.   *About one's self*

There are people who think that just because they were raised by a poor family, they will remain to live in poverty forever. Some of these individuals think that becoming wealthy is unlikely or too difficult for them to achieve. What is even worse, some have accepted their lives of living scantily, they do not want try to think of making something better with their lives. They have created a comfort zone and refuse to take risks by looking for new opportunities or starting a new business of their own.

11

b.   *About Money*

An old childhood express is, "money is the source of all evil" that people often forget or ignore aiming for greater wealth goals in their lives. It is not that one should focus all their attention on money, but as the common express is "if you fail to plan, then you are in effect planning to fail" when it comes to wealth accumulation.

3.   Material world

Marketing and advertising have ingrained materialism and consumerism in our minds. Through their convincing power and skills, we have been brain washed that a particular thing, such as a smartphone, is a "need "and not merely a "want."

4.   Parkinson's Law

This law states that "expenses rise to meet income." While salaries may increase, people may still find their income insufficient because of a corresponding increase in their expenses brought by their confidence that they can afford this time certain items or services that may not have been able to afford previously.

5. Comforts and privileges

The digital era has brought not only comfort and ease, but many temptations as well. With the emergence of online shopping and banking, one may conveniently make a purchase and pay for it without having the need to leave home and withdraw cash. This has created so many charges to one's account that increases balances on loans and credit cards for many people.

Chapter 3:
Earning, Saving, & Investing:
The Road to Becoming Wealthy

You surely do not want to spend the rest of your life working even until after the age of retirement. As somebody who grew up in a family that was a member of the "paycheck to paycheck society" before, I understand that most people look forward to that day when you no longer need to worry about your finances, i.e. - worrying if the cash in your wallet will is enough for the week, if the loan you have applied for will be granted just in time for the much-needed change of residence, or if you will get the promotion you are aiming for so there will be an increase in your salary.

There are only three sure ways by which you can accumulate wealth – by earning, saving, and investing. Let me warn you, however, that these three are easier read and said than done. It takes a lot of discipline, self-control, and determination to be able to make enough money, save some amount from that earnings, and put your resources into an investment.

14

1. Earning

Making enough money is the most fundamental among these three steps. There are two kinds of income – earned which is what you get with what you do for a living (as a businessman, skilled worker, or professional) and passive which you get through your investments.

I will generalize that people who want to be wealthy are just starting or are midway in their career, while I am writing this book. I will start with why earned income is important for this section.

To be able to earn enough, here are five things that you need to keep in mind:

a. Do what will make you qualify for a particular position – To land a position that you are aiming for, determine what will make you a good fit for it.

b. Do what keeps you interested – With your heart and mind set on a particular task or activity, things will be light, and although not necessarily easy, your interest will give you the push to accomplish more.

c. Do what you excel in – Put your talents and skills on jobs where they will be maximized and put to good use.

15

d. Do what will pay you well – You work to earn a living, so it's to your advantage if you focus on work that is financially rewarding.

e. Do what will give you enjoyment – You will be motivated to perform your best if you enjoy what you are doing.

All of the above items will help you to maximize your earnings, which is a key first step in wealth creation.

2. Saving

Now that you have maximized your earnings, your next step is to set aside a portion of your earnings in order to increase your passive income and earnings. The wrong notion is that saving should be your last priority when coming up with an allocation for your salary. What you should do is to think of yourself as your own employee and when your paycheck from your job has finally arrived, pay yourself first. You should start by saving 10% of your earnings, or perhaps an amount that is higher or lower, depending on what you can afford based on the budget you have already set for yourself. After that amount for your savings has been put aside, you pay your bills and life off what is left from that paycheck.

However, saving does not only involve taking a portion from your salary. As written earlier, it takes a lot of effort to keep yourself from spending and enjoying the "extra money" you have put away for savings. Due to this temptation, I have listed some helpful tips that will make saving easier for you. Moreover, I am citing some sound financial experiences and habits of known personalities who have been featured in the official website of AARP , an organization which aims to improve people's quality of life , in Investopedia , a site which gives education on investments and in the official site of Inc., the magazine which features growing companies.

a. ***Start early in life.***
   This is the idea behind orienting children, as young as they are, on the concept of saving thru their piggy banks. For those who did not develop the habit while growing up, now is the best time to start doing it. Don't' wait for your kids (or yourself) to get older to start saving. As a five year horizon is far too short for saving and investing if you want to become wealthy.

b. ***Think of yourself as not rich***. - *(I chose to never call myself poor – negative thoughts are not good in wealth creation.)*
   This will make you avoid unnecessary expenses and just spend on your basic needs.

17

This will also help you to resist many temptations and give up a lot of things in life, such as going out most of the time to eat, hanging out with friends, or going on a shopping spree.

Through this mind set, you should also set limits when it comes to your purchases such as buying clothes or shoes that are not more than $50, or finding cheaper substitutes for expensive cooking ingredients.

Alfred Morris, running back for the American football team Washington Redskins, actually has a four-year contract amounting to $2.2 million. While he can easily afford to buy an expensive car, Morris still drives a 1991 Mazda which he bought for $2 from his pastor when he was still a student. The famous billionaire investor Warren Buffett has told in many interviews that he still has is simple home in Omaha, Nebraska, rather than buy multiple expensive homes all over the place that just sit their empty doing nothing.

c. *When making a purchase, give it a lot of thought first.*
Many consumers are impulsive buyers (my sister). By asking yourself many times before bringing an item, especially a non-essential one, to the counter for payment,

18

"do I really need this? Or do I just want it? you are actually preventing yourself from buying something and then having regrets later that you bought it.

d. *Take advantage of automation*

Setup a direct and recurring transfer of funds from your checking account to a savings or an investment account. With this, you can be sure that you are regularly adding an amount to your savings. This will also give you a means of telling your brain you only spend money in this one checking account allocated for monthly expenses. All other money is "not touchable". Soon your brain will truly accept it and saving and investing will become automatic and multiply.

e. *Pay in cash, look for discounts, buy in bulk*

You will definitely be saving a lot by purchasing in cash as you avoid interests, charges and fees imposed when buying on instalment basis or through your credit card. Personally I rarely buy anything in cash though. I use a few credit cards for all my purchases and this credits all give me travel or hotel rewards so I can take vacations for free. The important thing is, I pay all my credits off every month!! I never ever let balances carry over from month to month. So essentially it is like using cash, but I "borrow money interest free" for up to 30 days (dependent on where you are in your credit card payment cycle when you purchase) and you are paying yourself back for a free vacation in the future. This take extreme discipline, that I do not recommend to beginners, so use a debit card instead to start out if do not want to "carry around cash", then you can make the transition later to a credit card.

Buying in bulk or wholesale can help you save as well compared to retail or buying by the piece, especially if you have children.

Use coupons and vouchers will also help you limited your spending and increase your savings. It has been reported that famous people like Lady Gaga, Carrie Underwood, Hilary Swank, and Kristen Bell, although they have a lot of money in the bank, are serious in their collection of coupons.

f. *Always choose quality over popularity*
Never mind what's trendy. Buy what will last a long time so you don't have to buy the same item over and over again. This is the belief of many wealthy people. Business magnate T. Boone Pickens once said in an interview that he doesn't go for anything cheap, although he is not a shopper. He is always on the look for the best product. In

20

fact, he has a pair of loafers which he got in 1957 and still wears them to this day. I am not T. Boone Pickens but I have resoled a few of my favorite pairs of shoes and loafer that still look good because I take care of them. The cost of resoling every few years is 1/3 to 1/5 the cost of replacing them, and I do not have to get sore feet breaking a new pair in any more.

3. Investing

When you have saved enough, a good way to make the most of it is to put it in an investment. You definitely need money to make money, but no matter how small you think your savings are, never underestimate its power.

My discovery of investment as a powerful tool to build wealth was actually an accident. I told you in the introduction how I started to save and invest in my 401K. Well how I learned to invest well (versus speculative investment), was a basic concept you may have heard many times. Invest in what you know. Yes, it is that simple. Let me give you two examples. I was working for a company, and as part of my work I looked at a few different competitive products. I thought they were good at the time. It was early in my investing career, so

21

I did a little research (I say little because I did not really know how to research well back then) and decided to buy 50 or 100 shares of these two different stocks. I did not have much spare money so I just bought the minimum I could afford. Over the next 5 years, the stocks grew and split, and I sold some shares after the split to get my initial investment back (something I also learned by talking to people in the hall – so Thankful to all my friends!!). They kept going up. Split a few more times, I sold a few more shares. I at least tripled my money. I tell you this because I bought what I knew. I have too many stories of buying what I did not know and losing money. The ones I bought that I knew more than made up for it. Now, I only buy what I know, which is a similar strategy that Warren Buffett uses, except he has lots of great people to research companies before he buys.

Putting your money into an investment does not stop there as there are four important things that I would like to share with you.

a. *Buy stocks instead of the product.*
   Instead of being just a buyer or consumer of a product, wouldn't you want to be a co-owner of a company which manufactures it? Take the case of

22

the Pop icon Madonna who was said to be just a daily consumer of Vita Coco, the coconut water, while on her music tour. In 2010, she decided to invest a hefty amount of $1.5 million together with other celebrities like Demi Moore, Matthew McConaughey, Anthony Kiedis and Red Hot Chili Peppers. Madonna bought what she knew and what she liked.

b. **Start your own business**
Instead of investing your savings in an existing firm, you may also choose to have start your own business. Well-known personalities like Lady Gaga and Kim Kardashian have been putting their money into their own businesses, a platform which connects music and sports celebrities to their fans and an on-line shoes and accessories website, respectively. My grandmother calls this investing in yourself. She always told us kids "you can never go wrong investing in yourself".

c. **Stay informed and updated**
Make it a habit to read finance books and journals (such as the Wall Street Journal and Forbes Magazine) and listen to finance experts, instead of turning the pages of fashion and gossip magazines.

23

Also, get a book on Finance that teaches you have to read the balance sheet, cash flow statements, quarterly, and annual reports of companies. This will help you make informed decisions when investing. Later will we review how to plan your investing comfort or risk level before deciding how much and what investments to make.

d. *Have as many income streams as possible.*

If you have the resources, have a diversified portfolio. This means that you will be putting your money into not just on one, but into several different investments. The former NBA star Magic Johnson can be an inspiration as he has done a lot since he stopped playing some 20 years ago. With his holding company, Magic Johnson Enterprises, his earnings are now derived from restaurants, movie theaters, stakes in real estate companies, life insurance companies, sports teams which are worth millions of dollars, and in Sodexo, the multinational food services and facilities Management Corporation based in Paris, France. Diversifying your portfolio is designed to reduce your overall investment risk. This goal of this is to increase your upside or growth of your

24

wealth while trying to minimize your downside or reduction in wealth.

Chapter 4:

Learn How to Manage Your Own Money

Now that you have learned how to begin to create your wealth, I would like to focus on the last of the three steps (and eventually the most important), which is investing. Before putting the money you have worked hard for and saved for to a better purpose, there are some factors that you need to consider. You have some decisions to make on where, how, and when to invest your savings. You need to evaluate a few key factors to come up with the best strategy for yourself when it comes to your investments. Here are some important criteria you need to weigh when coming up with the best strategy for yourself.

1. When to start

This is the most important factor. You have to decide when the right time is for you to start to invest.

Strategy:

26

a.   Ascertain that you have enough available cash to invest. If you are still paying off debt, it is generally a good principle to pay off consumer debit such as credit card debt first before investing your extra cash, as the loan interest may be higher than your potential earnings from an investment.

b.   Get insurance, such as good health and life insurance first, before investing so you can be spared from possible financial trouble if something goes wrong that will eventually wipe out the rest of your savings.

c.   Convert your discretionary expenses into investing. Never confuse your wants with your needs.

d.   When you have achieved these, then start your investment as soon as possible. The longer your money is invested, the better the chances for your investments to double and grow. All you need to have is patience and a strategy for you to have success and great returns.

2. Your Personal Investment Objective:

There are three different main objectives which you should consider:

a. *Conservative* – This is your objective to keeping the money safe so you can use it soon such as when one is nearing retirement

Strategy:

- First make sure you have saved enough cash so you can live for at least 12 months if any issues like a job loss occurs.

- After building an emergency cash reserve, investing in high-grade (not junk) bonds is a typical conservative strategy

- Investing in bonds can be complicated, so you need to do some homework, and you usually need a bond advisor when you first start out. You need to know how to determine the better rated bonds versus the poor quality bonds, and as a rule of thumb, stay with the top rated less risky bonds for investing.

b. *Moderate Risk* – Your objective here is to take a little risk because you have a longer time horizon or you feel you need a higher return on your investments.

Strategy:

- Invest in stable companies which pay dividends

28

- Invest in a blend of dividend paying stocks and enroll in the dividend reinvestment program to allow your money in that company's stock to grow over time

- Typically for a moderate risk investment, you invest in a mix of dividend stocks and bonds together.

c. ***Aggressive Growth*** – Your objective here is to take higher risk with the goal of getting higher growth/returns on your money.

Strategy:

- Investments that focus on growth of your investment, such as small capitalization (nick named small-cap) stocks that typically can grow very quickly.

- Remembering with the opportunity for high growth there is the higher risk of losing a significant portion of your initial investment.

- Balancing some middle capitalization (nick named mid-cap) stocks and even some large-cap stocks into your investment strategy to get a blend of stock price growth and dividend income.

29

- Typically aggressive growth investing does little bond investing, and less large-cap stock investing overall.

Whatever goal you may have, make sure to separate your objectives with your emotions. Setting your emotional attachment to a security or investment apart from your objective of ownership will lead you to better choices and performance.

It has also been my experience and the advice of many investment advisors to start with what you know. This will mean to look at stocks of companies that you are familiar with because it is in the same industry as the one you work in (without doing any illegal insider trading) or products that you use and buy every day for home or personal use. Then research those stocks before choosing which stocks to invest in.

3. Your Age

A person's age is a big factor when it comes to investing because it may dictate the kind of investment that you will be most appropriate for you. Basically, being young will work to an investor's advantage as you have a longer time to let your investments grow and "weather" unexpected losses in your investment portfolio. Older individuals just starting out investing, have to weigh the short time horizon with the need to protect their initial investment so they will have enough money to spend when they retire.

Strategy:

a. For those who are just starting out, a good start (like I did) is to sign up with your company's 401(k) program at your first job even for just the minimum amount.

b. For those who have recently been married, you may need some of your retirement funds for the purchase of a home. Remember that you have to save and invest at the same time.

c. For couples with young families, while you may still want to be aggressive with your investments in the stocks, remember to start college savings plans for your children's education. A good practice for families is to update your beneficiaries with your life insurance policy and retirement account(s).

d. People who are nearing retirement (in their 50s), invest in fixed incomes or bonds and dividend paying stocks.

e. Retirement age people, if you have high growth or mid to small capitalization stocks, you probably want to consider safer investments, but with some income generating dividend-paying stocks or bonds.

31

4. Understand Your Time Frame

This refers to the time you have before you intend to turn your investment into cash. It can be long-term, medium-term, or short-term.

Strategy:

    a. If you intend to stay invested for the long run, you may opt to take bigger risks since you will still have time to recover in case of some losses.

    b. If you don't have that much time, then choosing the less risky investments like high-grade bonds is a better choice.

5. Your Risk Tolerance

The general rule is that the higher the risk you take, the higher chances you have for bigger returns. It also can mean the higher risk for losing your initial investment.

Strategy:

    a. Invest in a business which you can understand. Investing in something which you don't understand will make it difficult for you to make sound decisions. Among the

32

easiest investments to make are those of index ETFs and index funds.

b. Avoid the most common mistake of people who think investing is about the product. Finding a "good investment" is actually a myth. What you should deal more with is your timing, strategy, and how you will handle the risks involved. It requires hard work, time, and effort in researching each investment.

c. If you are the aggressive type who can accept loss of money for the possibility of getting more growth (profit), you may choose to choose growth stocks such as mentioned in the aggressive growth section of "your personal investment objective".

d. If you feel you are more conservative, you either choose moderate risk or conservative investment objective. You may feel you are not comfortable with investing as you are afraid to lose any money, if that is the case it is okay as well.

e. It will be best to put your cash reserves and your investment in different savings/investing buckets. This will create a balance between the funds you will need in the future. I often open different accounts for my different investing and savings needs so as to make it more difficult to access the money for "compulsive want type purchases".

f. One way to diversify is to put some of your money into stocks, while the rest into bonds. You can also try investing into local and international stocks and to local and international bonds.

g. No matter what happens around you, just focus on what you have planned to do. Don't let the news about investment or stories from investors you know change your course of action.

h. Make small, infrequent adjustments to your strategy as investment is a long-term activity that needs gradual changes over time instead of immediate and abrupt changes.

Chapter 5:

Here are Your Steps to Take Next

In this book's final chapter, I would like to lay out clear steps that you can take now for you to get closer to that goal of accumulating wealth.

As it was earlier explained, people aim for wealth for three main reasons: for one's freedom (financial freedom), for fame and for power. To achieve financial success, your motivation should be for freedom, both personal and financial, and not necessarily with the goal to become famous nor to become powerful. To gain fame and power is but naturally tempting, but giving in to such desires can easily snatch away from you the wealth you have worked hard for.

As stated earlier also, to avoid living paycheck to paycheck, you need to begin by setting a reason budget to live on for yourself. The bottom line is to strengthen your self-discipline - live within your means, focus more on your needs and less on your wants. Negative thoughts about yourself and about money, in general, should be avoided. Stay focused on setting a goal and getting used to living on the budget until you have finally reached your ultimate goal.

The concrete ways leading to your accumulation of wealth – earning, saving, and investing were discussed. To begin to save, you have to have a plan for earning first. You will need to follow the guide given for you to increase your pay. Specifically you will have to put your interests, qualifications, talents, and satisfaction as priorities in making your choice for a job or source of living. On top of these, you will also have to consider the compensation or monetary gains before coming up with a decision. If your   present work or source of income does not meet such criteria, then you might as well look at changing your job or business.

After establishing a reasonable earning goal, most important in the steps is to save or as they say "pay yourself first". Saving should begin at the earliest stage of your profession or career, no matter how small it may be. If you haven't done it, then you should begin today. Saving a portion of your income should be your first move and not your last, the moment you receive your pay check. This is often best done by having the money go into an account that is not easy to access, no ATM or debit card access, no check writing. Just a high interest savings account where you actually have to physically go in to get money from the account is a great way to discipline yourself. Moreover, once you have started saving, live on that limited budget you set. Don't splurge just because you have the resources saved up for your whims and desires.

Finally, the last phase, investing, is your most powerful tool in accumulating wealth. The discussion about investing in Chapter 3 should have given you a better perspective on where you could possibly put your savings after you have set aside that portion of your income. From there, you need to start to draft a plan on where to invest your money.

In the preceding chapter, the factors to consider when coming up with a decision about how to begin investing were outlined. Together with the information are useful strategies to consider which you may adopt to start on your path to financial success. Study and adhere to the strategy that best suits you and complete your initial plan for investment by listing down the manner in which you plan to do it, in terms of the period when you should start, your objective, your present age, your time frame, and the risk that you are willing to take.

I have shared my personal experiences and learning about earning, saving, and investing with you. Remember that your success in investing, and eventually the attainment of your goal to accumulate wealth, still depends on you. What I have provided you here are pointers, but the action and the willingness to follow and pursue them still lie on you. There are risks to consider and I know I have made a few mistakes along the way, but even with mistakes I have gained more and learned more by staying focused on my personal wealth goal.

I hope the learnings I have shared with you have given you the motivation to at least do step 1) determine the necessary earnings for you and your family, and set a plan to change the plan if necessary as a family. Then step 2) pay yourself first and start saving. These two steps may take a few years to execute for you and your family, but they are the most important and best ways to secure a finance future. Step 3) is to begin to learn about investing, and now you should be motivated to learn more. Never lose focus on your financial goals and never stop learning. You can do it!!

Check Out Other Books

"Start Your Wealth Building Now: Your Next Steps to Investing Made Simple" – also by **Anthony R. Thomas**